"CAN'T" IS A FOUR-LETTER WORD

Creating Healthy Rebellion Against Roadblocks and Glass Ceilings of Potential

LAUREN DANIELLE

Positively Powered
positivelypoweredauthors.com

Editor: Amy Collette
Cover Design: Melody Christian

Why Can't Is A Four-Letter Word/Lauren Danielle. 1st ed.
ISBN 978-1-7329022-6-8

Acknowledgements

To Jon Cook, who first believed in me and empowered me to tell my story.
To Amy Collette, for your continued support and lovingly direct advice throughout the process.
To my champions for their unconditional support and encouragement.
To every experience life has given me that fueled me to say "I Can..." and therefore... You Can.

"If you're going to do something, give it your all or don't do it at all."

~ LAUREN DANIELLE

CONTENTS

CAN'T: Worst Four-Letter Word. Ever.................... 1

WHY CAN'T YOU?... 11

    Why You Say You Can't 12

    Why Other People Say You Can't 12

THE BRAIN BATTLE: Change Your Mind First,
Change Your Life Forever 15

    What You Believe Will Be 19

    Reshape Your Beliefs 20

MAKE THE SWITCH: Moving Your Brain From
"Can't" to "Can".. 23

CREATING HEALTHY REBELLION 29

ABOUT THE AUTHOR................................. 37

CAN'T: Worst Four-Letter Word. Ever.

It wasn't that long ago that I had zero time. I was working 80, 90, sometimes *100* hours a week as a group fitness professional, personal trainer, restaurant server, metabolic coordinator, membership director, fitness boot camp organizer, and clinical nutritionist.

Just typing all that feels exhausting. There was no time to just be me. I was wearing multiple hats, trying to do all sorts of things, none of which I loved, and none of which were providing the life I wanted.

I found myself emailing at night, texting clients while I was working out, skipping my workouts to pick up a shift at the restaurant, and constantly running around from one job to the next. Not to mention missing friends' birthdays and family holidays — all to simply make ends meet.

I was so frustrated with life. I wanted to help people in the health industry, not sell my precious time for a tiny paycheck. That's my passion, my big "why," as Simon Sinek would say. I have two Bachelor's degrees, two Master's degrees, (which were not cheap!) and was told I was only worth $12.00 an hour! I was so done with exchanging time for money. I knew I was meant for more.

Everything changed when I decided to go against all the odds and dive into a profession I knew nothing about, except that I thought I didn't like it. When I first got the call to take a look at a network marketing health and wellness company, I thought, "How much time do I need to give to this to make it work? What do I need most that network marketing can provide, that no other vehicle or "job" in my life can deliver? If I don't do this, what would life look like in ten years compared to if I do take this leap?"

In an extra hour a day, I chose to focus my efforts and bring my passion to changing my life, to making something come to fruition. I thought, "What's the risk? I can always wait tables, bartend, and train people, but where's the joy? Where's the freedom?"

If I didn't say yes, things couldn't get worse, and I already knew what that felt like. However, if I did say yes, I imagined how things could look different and decided there was only one way to go... up.

I want to share a little backstory of my life with you. I was always the black sheep, the only kid in the family who really got into trouble. I always heard, "Oh, what's Lauren going to do now?" and "Leave it to Lauren not to follow the rules."

I grew up with a lot of doubts, a lot of times the word "can't" was whispered in my ear and thrown in my face. "Lauren can't do this..." "Lauren can't do that..."

For example, I was constantly changing my major in college, not only as an undergraduate but also in graduate school. It was obvious I was noncommittal and searching for more. I was the sibling who rebelled, didn't get straight A's, and had one too many parent-teacher conferences. Simply put, my belief meter — knowing and trusting I could accomplish anything I set my mind to — was on low, if it was on at all.

Even if it wasn't deliberate, the disbelief I felt from others was always there.

Can't. Can't. Can't. It's suffocating, scary, and controls your greatest potential. The good news is that you can decide at any time whether you want to live your current story or write a new one. It starts with saying, "I can."

How could I do network marketing? I had zero sales experience, zero experience in leadership development, virtually zero experience in social media branding, and did I mention I had zero time?

I was brand-new to the industry, overwhelmed, stretched thin with time, and had an ongoing recording in my head about not being good enough. I felt everything was stacked against me. Everything about this opportunity screamed, "Lauren can't succeed."

And yet I said, "I'm going to make this happen!" Deep down I knew that if I wanted it badly enough I could make it happen. There were times in my life that I had made a decision to just go for it. If it was going to be, it was up to me.

It's always been my passion to do something significant and I had the burning desire to live on purpose, which has helped push me to greatness. "I can do this!"

I had to learn to succeed in this profession. After all my years in school, I found myself back *learning* the trades and skills of this industry to become the best I could be. I committed to putting in as much training and time as I possibly could to master this opportunity and to provide the best service to others.

I knew in my heart that this was the vehicle that could assist me in helping other people. Not only did I love health and wellness and I had found a company that aligned with my nutritional beliefs, but I fell in love with the vision of the company, the mission statement, and the core values. Additionally, I was so excited about the ability to partner with others. I saw how the compound effect of effort would directly change my income, and I knew that I would finally escape the trap of exchanging time for money.

I also believed in my heart this opportunity could help me reach the masses, as opposed to one by one in my tiny private practice nutritionist office. I also knew in my gut that an opportunity like this wasn't going to come around again in my lifetime (an alignment of quality products, a company with integrity, and compensation beyond measure), so the time was *now*! If I ever wanted time and financial freedom, I had to put my fears aside and believe that I could!

Network marketing focuses on five beliefs: belief in your industry, belief in your product, belief in your company, belief in the compensation, and belief in yourself. At first I was a skeptic, a huge skeptic. I wondered, "Will this really work? What will my clients think of me? What will my family think? Am I joining a pyramid scheme? Who's going to even listen to me? Why am I going to put my eggs in one basket when I don't even believe in this industry?"

It didn't take long to go from skeptic to ambassador, because I had found my niche, my true calling, and was seeing success. I was having so much fun meeting new people, developing new leaders, and being praised and recognized by my mentors and corporate support in ways I never had.

Something interesting happened, though. This was one of the first times the "can't" was actually coming from me, not anybody else. This was the first time I was challenging myself with the idea that I could have more in life and live a life where I was no longer exchanging time for money.

The fear I had was not of failure, but rather of success. It wasn't long before that I had felt stuck, limited, and trapped, and suddenly I was moving and shaking and visualizing in a bigger way than I had ever dreamed.

There's a saying that we don't grow in our comfort zone but rather when we are outside of our comfort zone, and that is exactly what was happening. The fear of letting others down, the fear of not knowing how to manage a six-figure income, and the fear of failing all crept into my mind and I had to decide to allow the reel of self-sabotage to play or the reel of empowerment, perseverance, and grit to shine through.

My close friends and my sister saw my burning desire to build a brighter future for myself and for others. When they saw what I was committed to doing and that I was on a relentless pursuit to better myself and others, they started joining me. I had a vision to build an empire. While some would call me an amateur or rookie, I knew I was devoted, and others believed in the dream I saw and the determination I had.

Now I'm bulletproof to the doubters. My "can't" is now "I did," and that fuels my passion to see others get rid of their "can't."

This is my manifesto, a call to push back against the word "can't." How many times have people told you that you didn't have what it takes? How many times have you told yourself you don't have what it takes? Who says you can't?!

It's all just stories... **You Can.**

This book is for you.

"The power of 'can't:' The word 'can't' makes strong people weak, blinds people who can see, saddens happy people, turns brave people into cowards, robs a genius of their brilliance, causes rich people to think poorly, and limits the achievements of that great person living inside us all." ~Robert Kiyosaki

---

WHY CAN'T YOU?

*"Only I can change my life. No
one can do it for me."*
~Carol Burnett

Who says you can't? The word "can't" can be so suffocating and restricting. It can be one of the most crippling words in everyday life because it automatically tells the world, "I quit on this opportunity," or "I'm not good enough."

Why You Say You Can't

Can't isn't always a bad word. Sometimes saying "can't" is a really liberating experience. By saying you "can't" do something, you're communicating that it's your choice not to pursue a less important priority or opportunity.

Why Other People Say You Can't

But people also use words like "can't" to tell you what *they* think you're capable of.

I wasn't supposed to graduate from high school. I had made poor choices, did not have enough credits, and found myself in a scary predicament just before my senior year. People even said, "Lauren can't graduate. She won't be able to graduate."

Not only did I graduate, but I graduated early! When I think about my childhood, anytime I was told "No" or "You can't," I took on a "Watch me now" mentality. I was born with determination and have always had the drive to do what it takes, in spite of my doubters.

So, where does "can't" come from? Sometimes people use "can't" because they don't want to believe in someone if they think they might fail.

Sometimes people use "can't" because they're jealous. They want to hold you back from reaching a level of success that they're personally not capable of or willing to achieve. Just one example is: how many women sabotage their friends when they are on a diet? Misery likes company. We can get so wrapped up wanting approval from others that we lose the true idea of who we are, what we are passionate about, and ultimately, what our purpose is.

If we listened to everyone who says we don't have what it takes, we would never take a risk. Don't let other people be the judge and jury of your potential.

If Nelson Mandela hadn't been able to forgive and have the vision he did, imagine how different the world would be. It takes one powerful leader to make a global impact.

Not everyone will agree with you and not everyone will support you, but when you know your drive is to impact others in a positive way and when you face yourself in the mirror and know you did your very best, there's no room for others to stand in your way.

The only reason you can't succeed is if you don't believe you can. The biggest question you need to answer is "**Why can't I?**"

"I can accept failure, everyone fails at something. But I can't accept not trying."
~Michael Jordan

THE BRAIN BATTLE: Change Your Mind First, Change Your Life Forever

When I worked as a personal trainer, the biggest challenge was rarely my client's physical limitations. It was usually their mindset that was the biggest problem. The body is often more than capable; however, your mind often stops you well before your body does. For example, no one believed a human could run a four-minute mile; however, once it was done, *many* went on to repeat it.

The biggest obstacle to success for so many people is the six inches between our ears. The stories we tell ourselves. We are born with two fears: falling and loud noises. This simply means that if everything else is learned, I believe it can also be unlearned.

When I set my mind to something, I'm very determined. My entire life is a series of times when I was a rebel, which is not always a good thing. As an early teen, I went against the grain but learned incredible lessons when I turned my life around and graduated from high school early.

I decided to be self-employed (prior to network marketing) instead of choosing standard corporate jobs. While I was a "joke" to many, meaning I couldn't stay committed to one thing, was always on to something different, or I appeared to be a lost and wandering soul, I've always had good instincts and a vision of success that has led me to today.

I found myself in my twenties with no social life, working ludicrous hours, and feeling completely unfulfilled. I knew something needed to change. I was willing to go all out to change the status quo of my chaotic, unpredictable life. Maybe I wanted to prove people were wrong about me, but my real motivation was getting in my own mind and proving to myself that I had what it takes to succeed. I was afraid of my financial future. Would I be able to experience financial freedom if I continued down the road I was on? Would I be able to help the people I wanted to? Would I miss out on precious time with my friends and family?

All of us are capable of so much more when the desire to change exceeds our doubt that we can change.

Is the pain of staying where you are greater than the pleasure of being comfortable and playing it safe? If so, that is when I believe you can make mountains move.

It seems to me that we're almost afraid of our own potential. When I talk to people now, they give me objections about why they think they don't have what it takes to succeed. Often the fear is newness or unfamiliarity. "I've never done this before," or "I don't have the experience or the money or the resources." "This can't happen because I don't have the right people to make it work, enough time, or enough training."

What You Believe Will Be

Here's what I know: Whatever you believe will be. If you tell yourself you can't, you're right. This won't work as long as you defeat yourself in your mind before you even give yourself a chance to try. I think about how many times Edison "failed" with the light bulb before he succeeded. Or how many times Babe Ruth struck out before earning the home-run record. As Wayne Gretzky says, "You miss 100% of the shots you didn't take." At the end of the day, you *can* do anything you set your mind to, with hard work, dedication, perseverance and grit, and the willingness to fail forward.

Reshape Your Beliefs

We need to reshape our brains to see how many incredible opportunities are out there and that we have all the capability to seize those opportunities.

Since birth, we've all been conditioned. We've been shaped and molded, defined, had our self-worth capped by a salary or society, and fallen into patterns based on job titles, family roles, societal measures, and a whole bunch of other labels that lie about who we are.

Changing our thinking is the uphill battle, but acting on those opportunities is so much easier with the right mindset in place. Switching your brain from "I can't" to "I can" takes intentional curating of your thoughts, blocking out objections based in control and fear, and seizing the new opportunity to fully embrace your potential. It all starts with winning the battle for your mind.

You are capable of doing anything you want as long as you see it, believe it, and are willing to do whatever it takes to get there.

"Never say that you can't do something, or that something seems impossible, or that something can't be done, no matter how discouraging or harrowing it may be; human beings are limited only by what we allow ourselves to be limited by our own minds. We are each the masters of our own reality; when we become self-aware to this: absolutely anything in the world is possible.

Master yourself, and become king of the world around you. Let no odds, chastisement, exile, doubt, fear, or ANY mental virus prevent you from accomplishing your dreams. Never be a victim of life; be its conqueror." ~Mike Norton

MAKE THE SWITCH: Moving Your Brain From "Can't" to "Can"

How do you change your mentality from "I can't" to "I can?" What are some practical ways to start rewriting your mindset to take control and live an empowered life?

Here are a few simple ways you can start rewiring your brain to embrace new opportunities:

➤ Limit the negative narrative in your life. If it doesn't add value, hope, grace, peace, or positivity, don't let it in your mind!

➤ Get rid of people who don't add value or support to your life, or even worse, add drama or sabotage your dreams. Don't answer their phone calls or respond to their messages. Delete them from your social media and don't feel guilty for letting go of people who hold you back or bring you down.

➤ Surround yourself with people who bring out the best in you. As the saying goes, you are the sum of the five people you surround yourself with. If you want to be fit, hang out with athletes. If you want to be kind and giving, partner with individuals who are driven by contribution. If you want to become financially free, spend time learning from others who have found financial freedom. Success breeds success.

➤ Focus on what you have instead of what you don't have. I have so many things to be grateful for. Every day I choose to focus on what I have as opposed to what I don't have. Sometimes it is important to remember that "enough is enough," especially when you're on a path to strive for more. Even when I was living in an unfurnished apartment, I needed to remind myself I wasn't living on the street! Even when food isn't exactly what I expect at a restaurant, I have gratitude for the meal and the experience. Having gratitude is the key to happiness and success.

➤ Recognize your situation and make the choice to value every blessing as it comes your way. From the big things to the small things, pay attention to each blessing to make a difference in someone else's life. Our lives are richer and more cherished when we can add value to others. Instead of focusing on what others can't do, focus on what they are doing right and what you can recognize, acknowledge, and celebrate!

➤ Be open to new opportunities when they come your way. People are given opportunities every day, but often we are too busy or our heads are too stuck in the sand to see them. I love the saying, "When one door closes, another door opens," and this is a mantra I live by. Random acts of kindness are a great example of embracing new opportunities. Are you ready to say "yes" to exciting, even intimidating opportunities to do something great? Are you ready to embrace each day knowing you will attract in greatness? It starts with you.

➤ Be open to changes, including changing your environment. My mentality changed when my environment changed. If you're stuck with a flood of voices telling you what they think you're incapable of doing, you need to find a new environment to pursue healthy relationships with people who celebrate your potential and let go of those that are holding you back.

➤ Limit distractions and delay gratification for a greater purpose. Success is built on commitment and focus on what you want *most* rather than what you want now. Do you have the discipline and maturity to say "No" to distractions so you can focus on building something significant for tomorrow? I often ask myself what matters more: the next five minutes or the next five years?

➤ Changing your habits changes your life. Set weekly and monthly goals, not just New Year's resolutions. Create a detailed, measurable, and realistic set of goals to shoot for this year and keep track of your progress. I am an advocate of vision boards, SMART goals, and accountability partners. The subconscious mind is powerful. If we are used to doing things a certain way, even if it isn't serving us, it is critical that we retrain our thinking and find new habits that not only serve us but lead us to our dreams.

Climbing a mountain is about knowing what steps you need to take to get to the summit. Once you reach the summit, climb to the next one.

As soon as we stop striving for what we are working towards, everything we don't want in our lives shows up. A good friend once told me the peak is a very narrow spot, so if we don't keep striving for greatness, we quickly slide back down.

CREATING HEALTHY REBELLION

For years I worked as a personal trainer, group fitness leader, and clinical nutritionist. I heard more people tell me that they "can't" more than I could ever count! "I can't work that hard! I can't stick to my diet. I can't lose this weight! I can't teach that many classes!"

It's so heartbreaking to see people hit mental roadblocks and fall way short of their potential because they've been told they didn't have what it takes or they don't believe in themselves.

When you eliminate the restrictions of "can't," your entire outlook changes. It's a new awakening, like breaking free from shackles on your mind and heart.

When I reflect on past years, I can recall feeling so dissatisfied with how people were responding to me as I walked through the grocery store, as I walked in the gym, or even when I walked into my own office. I put off so much negativity that it was visibly affecting how people walked around me and engaged with me throughout everyday life. I felt as if people were moving away from me as opposed to moving towards me.

I am sure you can think of a time you could tell someone was in a hurry or they had such a chip on their shoulder you couldn't get out of their way fast enough. Unfortunately, and for many years, that was me. When I decided to slow down, embrace gratitude, to let go of what wasn't ideal and focus on what was going well, things started to change. Not only did my relationships change, but my health, my business, my finances, and my overall energy changed.

You can be anyone you want to be, so choose how you show up. My life coach used to tell me, "We slide to small or rise to big," and I vowed to never play small.

Now everything has changed!

I'm a magnet now because my energy output is different. My whole perspective has shifted and it's opening up new doors and conversations. I embrace life with gratitude and cheer. People gravitate towards me because they are hungry for that in their own lives. People are seeking hope and fulfillment. I created healthy rebellion against all the ways I wasn't supposed to succeed.

When you break free from your own inhibitions, you experience new possibilities and opportunities you would never have experienced if you had stayed inside the limitations of "can't."

I saw "can" come to fruition as it built my new belief:

➢ In less than 30 days I went from $17 to my name to having a fully furnished apartment and improved cash flow.

➢ In less than three months I was debt free (from college loans and poor credit card choices when I was living paycheck to paycheck), I had purchased a new car, and I was able to spoil my loved ones through the holidays.

➢ Within six months of super hard work, I quadrupled my income, retired from my practice, and was no longer exchanging time for money. I was experiencing time freedom, contributing more than ever, and embracing more love and serenity in my life than ever before.

I was living! And so can you!

If I can succeed, so can you. This is your chance, your time to shine. Take the old lies of people trying to control and limit your potential and turn that narrative into "I can do this!" What do you want most and what are you willing to do or to give up in order to succeed?

You need to find your place of suffering, the area of your life where you've heard "can't" more than any other word. Maybe it's your diet. Maybe it's your schedule. Maybe it's relationships. Maybe it's your business or finances or health or kids or career or family or free time or whatever.

If you found your opportunity to transform your place of pain, would you take it? If there was a way to improve your life, break free from misery, and welcome joyfulness, would you embrace that opportunity?

If you have fear of your potential, what's driving that fear? Is it fear of failure or fear of success? Is it fear of what others may think?

Embrace your full potential. Break out of your limitations. Be a rebel against the odds. Use this manifesto to say, "Who says I can't? I've got what it takes to be a success!" I often think of the *Little Engine That Could*... "I think I can... I think I can... I think I can..." and then **you can!**

My wish for you is to join me in healthy rebellion against the "can't" in your life. We can do this together. We can push against the lies and suppression of peoples' voices and our minds telling us we don't have what it takes. They're wrong and we're going to prove it.

You are worth it!

"*Often times our greatest fear is not the fear of failure; it's the fear we might actually be a big f***ing deal*" ~Author Unknown

WHO'S WITH ME?

ABOUT THE AUTHOR

Lauren Danielle is an industry leader in health and wellness, a commander in personal development, a nationally recognized speaker and trainer, and the author of *Get Off The Curb: A Healthy Rebellion From Fight or Flight to Activated Achiever*. Lauren's greatest passion is helping people break through physical, financial, emotional, and time barriers in order to live their fullest life possible.

She has undergraduate degrees in both psychology and sociology, dual master's degrees, over 15 years of experience in both her coaching and clinical practices, and has mentored and advised a variety of professionals, including top corporate executives, other entrepreneurs, and passionate individuals who want to make an impact or leave a legacy for others.

Lauren is an incredibly inspiring writer, speaker, and leader, pushing you to reach what you once thought was impossible. Lauren is so easy to relate to, you will find your story in her voice and be compelled to go out and take action in your own life!

Connect with Lauren at:
lifewithlaurendanielle.com

CPSIA information can be obtained
at www.ICGtesting.com
Printed in the USA
LVHW081041270219
608763LV00017B/14/P